Graphing Across the Curriculum

by Valerie Williams & Tina Cohen

SCHOLASTIC
PROFESSIONAL BOOKS

New York • Toronto • London • Auckland • Sydney

Acknowledgments

Grateful acknowledgments to Terry Cooper and the Scholastic staff for the opportunity to undertake this project. I could not have done it without the support of the administration, staff, parents, and students of the E. M. Baker Elementary School in Great Neck, New York.

Many thanks to my husband, Sam, and my son, Scott, for their patience and support. Thanks also to Mary Beth Spann for the encouragement to write. And special thanks to my first and best teacher, my mom.

V. W.

To my parents for your enduring faith and confidence. Special thanks to my best friend, my husband, Gene. To my children, Aaron and Ilene, you have taught me well.

T. C.

Cover design by Vincent Ceci and Jaime Lucero
Cover illustration by Elliott Kreloff
Interior design by Robert Dominguez and Jaime Lucero for GrafiCo Design
Interior photographs by Valerie Williams and Tina Cohen
Interior illustrations by Teresa Anderko

ISBN # 0-590-53551-X

12 11 10 9 8 7 6 5   8 9/9

Table of Contents

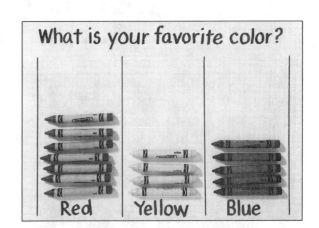

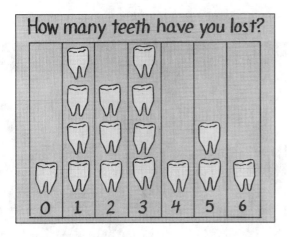

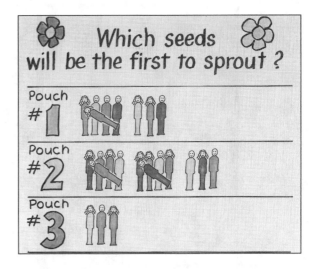

Table of Contents

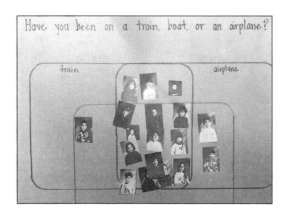

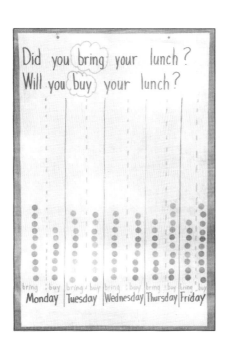

Introduction

Graphing has always been a part of our primary curriculum. Through the years, we have seen the many benefits of graphing activities. However, the real proof of graphing's value comes from our kindergarten and first-grade students themselves. At the end of a full year of graphing activities, we find that the children have begun thinking graphically. They eagerly suggest new ideas for graphs: "Can we make a tally graph of how many children like frogs and how many like toads?", "How about a 'Do you like to read' graph?" First graders are independently making graphs as a free-choice activity, answering questions such as, "What is the first letter of your first name?"; "What is your favorite kind of bird?"; "What is your lucky number?"; and even, "Which do you like better—pizza or Bart Simpson?"

Primary children are often introduced to graphs during math lessons. Through graphing activities, children learn to sort, classify, count, compare, organize, predict, and problem solve. But the mathematical skills taught through graphing can be applied to all curriculum areas. The reflective and analytical thinking fostered by graph-making enhances studies in science, language arts, literature, and social studies, as well as math.

This book includes dozens of ideas for graphing across the curriculum. Some can be used to introduce a lesson or to begin a unit of study, initiating focused discussions about the topics and allowing children to share prior knowledge and experiences. Other graphs can be used as culminating activities to wrap up a unit of study. And some graphs serve as assessment tools to measure learning and understanding of a particular concept or skill.

The classroom-tested graphs in this book cover a variety of formats: object graphs, picture graphs, symbol graphs, Venn diagrams, pie graphs, and bar graphs. Each activity follows this sequence:

- The **Graph Question** sets the purpose for making the graph.
- **About the Lesson** includes suggestions on how to use the graph and integrate it into your curricular studies.

- **Materials** list what's needed to create the graph.
- **Making the Graph** takes you step-by-step through the construction of the graph.
- **Reading the Graph** suggests questions to ask children once you've completed the graph.
- **Teaching Tips** offers classroom-tested ideas for extending the lesson.
- **Variations** suggest ideas for creating graphs in a related format or on a related topic.
- **Supporting Literature** recommends books related to the graphing theme.

This book also includes reproducible patterns to use in preparing the graph surface or as manipulatives on the graph. In addition, you'll find a photo of each completed graph to show you the variety of ways that the information can be displayed (on a bulletin board, as background for learning center activities, as a reference chart, and so on). You, of course, may choose to record and display the information in other ways.

As you complete the graphs, you're sure to pick up some techniques and strategies that will prove helpful in creating future graphs. The following hints may make your graphing experiences more successful:

- When preparing the graph surface, lay out the pieces to be sure that any manipulatives you are using will fit within the space allowed.
- Rows and columns on the graph should be sufficiently large to allow all students to make the same selection or prediction (which will rarely happen, but it's best to be prepared!).
- Look for commercially prepared ruled pads which provide a quick and easy graphing surface.
- Look for magazines or coloring book pictures to use as graphics.
- Use an overhead or opaque projector to enlarge graphics as needed.
- When possible, laminate the graph surface and/or manipulatives for repeated use.

All of the graphs in this book can be adapted to suit your curriculum needs and your students' ability levels. You may already have made graphs related to some of the topics included here. But we hope that you'll find some new ideas about how to present the information.

The use of graphs in our kindergarten/first-grade classroom has been insightful, educational, and fun! We hope your experience will be just as positive.

Valerie Williams
Tina Cohen

Chapter One

Object Graphs

These graphs use three-dimensional objects on a graphing surface.

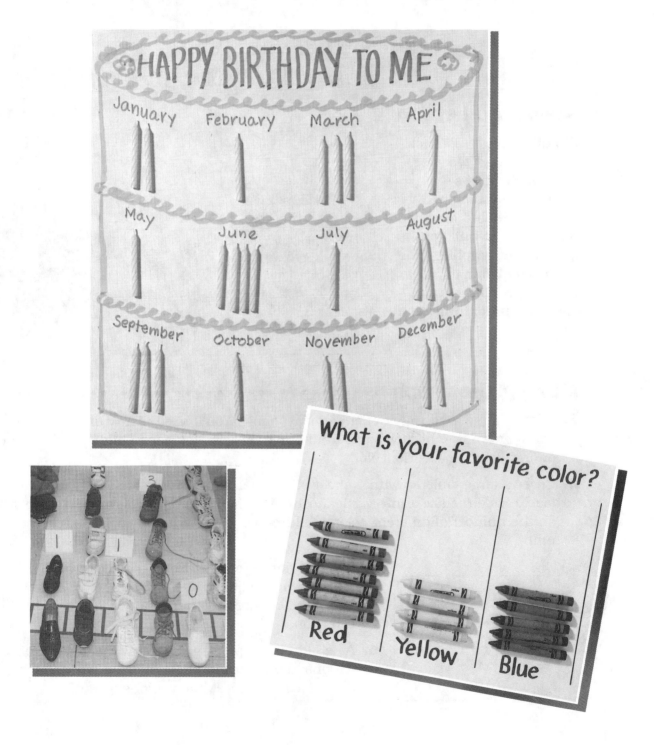

Crazy About Colors

About the Lesson

Children love to list their favorite things: foods, movies, TV shows—you name it. And tapping their special likes and interests is a good way to build excitement about graphing. You can use crayons to create this simple object graph showing students' favorite colors.

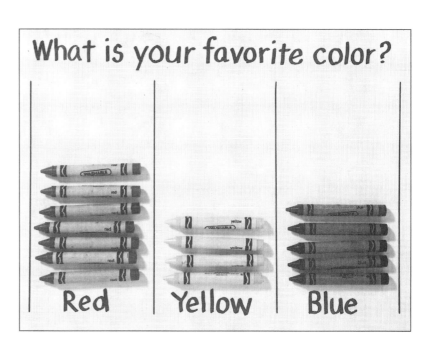

Making the Graph

1. Make a large assortment of crayons available. You'll need plenty of each color, so you may want to borrow some from other classes. Ask each child to pick a crayon in his or her favorite color.

2. Cover a large tabletop with a sheet of butcher paper. To create the graph surface, divide the sheet into vertical columns (the number of columns will depend on the number of different colors children choose). Write one color on each column.

Materials
- Crayons
- Butcher paper
- Marker

3. Invite children to come to the table one by one and place their crayons in the appropriate column. Invite the children to share the reason for their selection.

4. As children are placing their crayons, ask for observations about the changing information on the graph, for example, which color's ahead?

Reading the Graph ··········

- Which color was selected the most? The least?

- Was there any color that was not selected?

- Were any two or more colors selected by the same number of children?

- Are there two or more colors that we can add together to equal a third color? Can you find other combinations?

- What could people learn about our class's favorite colors by looking at the graph?

Variations ···················

- During a unit on weather, have students graph their favorite *rainbow* color. Paint a large rainbow on mural paper. Invite children to write their names or paste pictures of themselves in their favorite color on the arc of the rainbow.

- Try making color-related object graphs with autumn leaves, jelly beans, M&M's.

- Create "favorites" graphs in other formats. Some themes to try include dinosaurs, books, sports, types of fruit, school subjects, holidays.

Teaching Tips

- If children are choosing from a wide assortment of crayon colors, you may want to have them group their choices into color "families" on the graph, such as all the shades of green in one column, shades of blue in another, and so on.

- To introduce this activity, make a color wheel and allow children to experiment with mixing primary colors to create secondary colors. Children may also enjoy exploring color values. Divide the class into groups, and ask each group to pick a color. Challenge groups to come up with as many shades of their chosen color as possible by mixing it with varying amounts of white and black. Have groups create color charts to present their work to the rest of the class.

Supporting Literature

Is It Red? Is It Yellow? Is It Blue? by Tana Hoban (Greenwillow Books, 1978)

Mouse Paint by Ellen Stoll Walsh (Harcourt, Brace, Jovanovich, 1989)

Hailstones and Halibut Bones, a collection of poems about colors, by Mary O'Neill (Doubleday, 1961)

What's on Your Feet?

Graph Question: *What kind of shoes are you wearing today?*

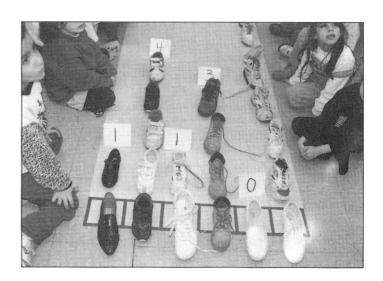

About the Lesson

This graphing activity will encourage students to hone their observation and classification skills by carefully examining the differences in their footwear. This graph works nicely as part of a social studies unit on clothing. You might also introduce it during a unit on transportation when you discuss travel by foot.

Making the Graph •••••••••••

1. Lay the butcher paper on the floor in an open area. The sheet should be several yards long to allow for all possible footwear combinations.

2. Mark off six long columns on the butcher paper (see photograph). Now draw horizontal lines to divide the columns into boxes. Each box should be large enough to accommodate a child's shoe. (The boxes will make it easier for children to visualize the results of the graph.)

3. Place a different shoe at the base of each column. The shoes will serve as labels for the different categories represented on the graph.

4. Invite students to sit around the graph. Ask each child to remove one of his or her shoes and decide which shoe represented on the graph most closely resembles it. Each child can then place his or her shoe in a box in the appropriate column on the graph.

Materials

- Large sheet of butcher paper
- Marker
- One each of the following types of shoes: tie, Velcro, tie/Velcro combination, slip-on, buckle, boot or sandle (or pictures of each shoe type)
- Blank file cards

5. After students have completed the graph they can tally the number of shoes in each column and write the totals on file cards. Set the file cards at the end of each row.

Reading the Graph • • • • • • • • • • • • •

- How many children wore sneakers? Shoes? Boots?

- How many children wore lace sneakers? Velcro sneakers? Slip-on sneakers?

- How many more wore tie sneakers than Velcro sneakers?

- Did fewer children wear sneakers or shoes?

- Did more children wear buckle shoes or slip-on shoes? *(substitute other shoe types)*

Variations •

- Try this activity using other articles of clothing, such as mittens and gloves, hats, or coats.

- T-shirts are a great theme for a graph. Designate a "T-shirt Graph Day" on which children should wear their favorite T-shirts to class. Ask them to decorate a simple T-shirt pattern (cut from paper) to resemble the T-shirt they are wearing. Students can then graph their T-shirt patterns according to the predominant feature (solid color, striped, with writing, picture only, school shirt, camp shirt, and so on). Enlist children's help in determining the categories for the graph. You might also want to try this activity using shoe patterns instead of real shoes. (See reproducible page 12 for clothing patterns.)

Supporting Literature

New Blue Shoes by Eve Rice (The Trumpet Club, 1975)

New Shoes for Silvia by Johanna Hurwitz (Scholastic Inc., 1993)

Shoes from Grandpa by Mem Fox (The Trumpet Club, 1989)

Clothing Patterns

Getting to Know You

Graph Question: *What color are your eyes?*

About the Lesson

In this activity, children construct a "Getting to Know You" cube on which they record various information about themselves, such as eye color, hair color, height, and so on. The graph is an excellent beginning-of-the-year-icebreaker to get children acquainted with one another. It's also good for an "All About Me" unit. You can use the six-sided cube for a full week's worth of graphing activities!

Making the Graph

1. Provide each child with a copy of pages 15 and 16 and the materials needed to make the cube. Work through the steps together.

2. Assemble children with their completed cubes near a surface that can be written on, such as the chalkboard or a chart pad. Ask children which side of the cube they'd like to graph first. Our class decided to begin with the graph question, "What color are your eyes?"

3. Let the children write the graph question at the top of the chart paper, and the category names (brown eyes, blue eyes, hazel eyes, etc.) in a row along the bottom.

Materials

- Directions and materials for making the cube (see reproducible page 15)
- Labels for each side of the cube (see reproducible page 16)
- Chart paper
- Marker

4. Have children use the cubes to answer the graph question. They can stack the cubes on top of one another to form the columns of the graph. You can randomly call children to the graph to stack their cubes in the appropriate group or call children according to eye color ("Anyone who has blue eyes come and stack your cube. . . brown eyes. . . ," etc.).

5. Ask children to count the number of cubes in each column. Write the totals on the chart paper at the top of each column. You and your students can decide whether to continue graphing each of the other sides of the cube on the same day or at another time.

Reading the Graph ••••••••••••••••••••••••••••••••••••••

- What color eyes do the children in our class have?

- What is the total number of children who have brown eyes? Blue eyes?

- Do any children have green or hazel eyes? How many?

- Can we add any of the eye color groups together to equal another eye color group on the graph?

- Which eye color is the most common? The least common? Do you think this is true in all classes in the school?

Variations •••••••••••••••••••

- Try stacking the cubes in different ways to share the information recorded on the other sides of the cube. For example, you may want to stack them horizontally against the chalkboard, on chart pad, or on the floor.

- The cubes can be used in countless other ways for graphing activities. Use them to record class favorites. Pick a different category for each side, such as Who's your favorite author, song, TV character, type of cereal, holiday, day of the week, and so on. (See page 9 for more ideas on graphing "favorites.") Children can also paste pictures of animals, plants, vehicles, etc., onto the different sides of the cube and use them for a variety of picture-graphing activities. (See Chapter 2 for more on picture graphs.)

Teaching Tips

- Every child will need a cardboard milk or juice container, so you may want to start collecting them a couple of weeks prior to the day you plan to make the graph. Assembling the cube makes a nice take-home activity. Send the directions home with children so they can make the cube with a family member.

- If possible, put weighted objects (rocks, marbles, beans) into the cubes before sealing and covering them. This will make the cubes easier to balance when stacked to form graphs.

- Younger children can draw pictures instead of writing information on the cubes.

What You Do ●●●●●●●●●●

1. Use a marker to draw a line around the milk or juice container $3\frac{3}{4}$ inches up from the base. This will form the four square sides of the cube.

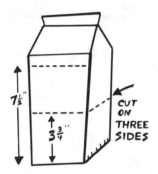

2. Measure up an additional $3\frac{3}{4}$ inches on one side of the container.

3. On three sides of the container, use a scissor to cut the line made by the marker in step 1. On the fourth side, cut at the $7\frac{1}{2}$-inch mark.

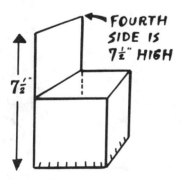

Materials

- Half-gallon milk or juice container
- Ruler
- Scissors
- Crayons/markers
- Art paper
- Tape/glue

4. Fold over the extended piece of cardboard and tape it in place to form the top of the cube.

5. Cover the cube with colored paper using tape or glue.

6. Fill in the information on the labels on page 16. Cut out the labels and glue one onto each

My name:

My age:

My height in inches:

The country (or state) I was born in:

My eye color:

My hair color:

Happy Birthday to Me!

Graph Question: *In what month were you born?*

About the Lesson

Birthdays are always cause for excitement in the classroom. They also present some fun graphing opportunities. In this lesson, children place birthday candles on a graphing surface to indicate the month in which they were born. You can use this activity to help familiarize children with the names and order of the calendar months.

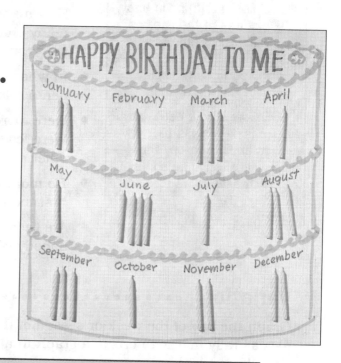

Making the Graph

1. Use an overhead projector to enlarge the birthday cake graph pattern on page 19 and draw it on the tag board.

2. Cut out the large cake shape and invite children to decorate it with paints and other art materials. Lay the cake graph flat on a table.

3. Gather students around the graph surface and give each child a birthday candle.

4. Ask children to name the month in which they were born. Have them place their candles on the graph next to the appropriate month.

Materials

- Birthday cake pattern (see reproducible page 19)
- Large piece of tag board
- Overhead projector
- Markers
- Scissors
- Paints and other art materials
- Birthday candles (one for each child)
- Self-sticking note paper (2-by-1½-inch size)

Teaching Tips

- Tape the candles in place on the graph. Staple the cake pattern to a bulletin board. Ask children to bring in baby pictures of themselves. Hang the pictures around the graph for a bulletin board display with a birthday theme.

- Follow up the activity by making a class birthday calendar showing the date of each person's birthday.

5. Invite volunteers to count up the number of children born in each month. Write the totals on self-sticking notes and attach them next to each month.

Reading the Graph ••••••••••••••••••

- How many children were born in March? How many children were born in the seventh month of the year? *(substitute other months)*

- In what month(s) does the greatest number of students celebrate their birthday?

- Were more children born in October or in June? Were fewer born in August or in April? *(substitute other months)*

- Do more children celebrate their birthday in the first month of the year or the last?

- Are there any months on the graph in which nobody celebrates a birthday?

Variation ••••••••••••••••••••••••••••••••••••

Graph the day of the week or season of the year children were born. Use the candles as tally marks to create a graph in a different format. (See chapter 3 for more on tally graphs.)

Supporting Literature

Arthur's Birthday by Marc Brown (Little, Brown, 1989)

On the Day You Were Born by Debra Frasier (Harcourt, Brace, Jovanovich, 1991)

HAPPY BIRTHDAY TO ME!

January   February   March   April

May   June   July   August

September   October   November   December

Chapter Two

Picture Graphs

These graphs use pictures to represent real objects or ideas on a graphing surface.

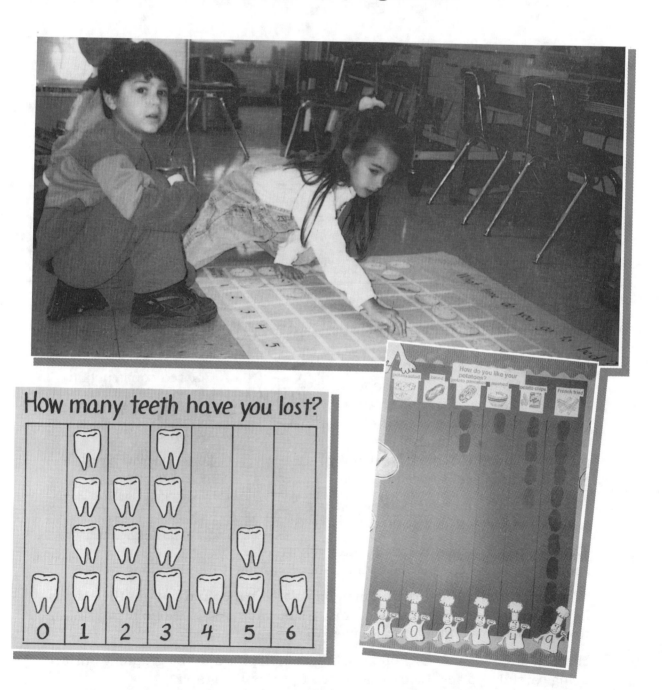

Left and Right

Graph Question: *Are you right-handed or left-handed?*

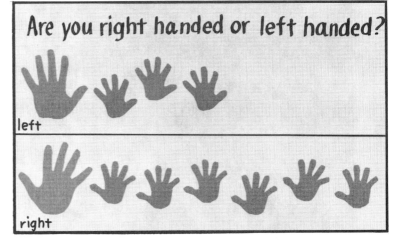

About the Lesson

Here's a very simple graphing activity to introduce children to picture graphs. This graph offers a fun way to reinforce the concept of left and right as children make and graph their own handprints.

Making the Graph

1. Ask children if they are left-handed or right-handed. Right-handed students should trace their right hand on a piece of colored construction paper. Left-handed students should trace their left hand. You may want to have children use one color of construction paper for right-hand prints and another for left, to visually reinforce the difference between the two.

2. Have children write their names on their handprints and cut them out.

Materials

- Colored construction paper
- Markers
- Scissors
- Long, narrow sheet of mural paper
- Tape/glue

3. Tape the mural paper to a wall. Draw a horizontal line across the middle of the paper to divide it into two long rows.

4. Trace your own left and right hands on colored paper and cut out the shapes. Label these shapes "Left-handed" and "Right-handed." Glue one handprint in front of each row on the mural paper.

5. Have children take turns gluing their own handprints to the graphing surface, being careful to place them in the correct part of the graph.

Reading the Graph ••••••••••••

- How many children are left-handed?
- How many children are right-handed?
- Are fewer children left-handed or right-handed?
- How many more children are right-handed than left-handed?
- From the graph, lead children to draw conclusions about which is more common, right-handedness or left-handedness.

Variations ••••••••••••••••••••••••

- Instead of tracing their handprints onto paper, children can cover a hand with tempera paint and make a print of it on art paper. Use these prints to make the graph.
- For a fun twist on this activity, invite children to find out if they are "right-footed" or "left-footed" by seeing which foot they step forward with first. Graph the results using footprints.
- As a take-home assignment, have children create mini-graphs showing which members of their family are right-handed and which are left-handed. Ask children to compare these graphs and try to draw conclusions about whether "handedness" runs in families.

Teaching Tips

- Some children may be ambidextrous; if so, include a section on the graph for these students. Mark the section with both a left and right handprint. Be sure all children understand this concept.

- Children may want to have visitors to your classroom add their handprints to the graph. Are most of the visitors left-handed or right-handed?

Families Big and Small

About the Lesson

Many early childhood curriculums include a study of the family. This graph will help children appreciate different family compositions. Introduce the graph by reading a story about a family. For this graph, we read the book *Families Are Different* by Mina Pellegrini. Use the book as a springboard for children to discuss their own families.

Making the Graph

1. Ask children to draw a portrait of their family. Their pictures should include all of their family members. Have students record their family surname on sentence strips and use the strips to label their pictures.

2. Invite children to share their illustrations and consider how they can be grouped. Suggest that they organize the illustrations according to the number of members in the family if no one mentions this possibility.

3. Have children determine how many people are in their family. Then group the pictures accordingly. Color-code each group of pictures by mounting them on different backgrounds (such as two-mem-

Materials

- 10-by-13-inch white drawing paper
- 11-by-14-inch colored paper
- Crayons/markers
- Sentence strips
- Glue
- Hole puncher
- Yarn or string
- Clothesline and clothespins

ber families could be mounted on red paper, three-member families on yellow, four-member on green, etc.).

4. Punch holes in the corners of each mounted picture. Use yarn or string to tie together the pictures mounted on the same color background in a ladder-like formation (see photo).

5. Hang the picture chains side-by-side from a clothesline to form the graph. Have students make sentence strips to identify the number of family members in each group of pictures ("There are _____ people in my family.")

Teaching Tip

Be sure that your discussion about families sensitively addresses different family structures (extended family, single parent family, step families, etc.).

6. Hang the sentence strips from the clothesline between the picture chains to define the "columns" of the graph.

7. Enlist children's help in creating a banner displaying the graph question "How many people are in our families?" Hang the banner over the clothesline graph.

Reading the Graph ••••••••••••••••••••••••••••••••••••••

- What is the smallest family group? What is the largest?

- How many children have two people in their family? Three people? Five?

- Do more children have three family members or four family members? (*substitute other numbers*)

- Do fewer children have two family members or five family members? (*substitute other numbers*)

- Can we add any two groups on the graph together to equal a third group?

Variations ••

- Children may want to graph the number of sisters and/or brothers that they have. They can also graph the number of aunts, uncles, or cousins in their family.

- Try the same graph format for an activity centering on family pets. How many children have pets? What kinds of pets do they have?

Supporting Literature

Families Are Different by Nina Pellegrini (Scholastic Inc., 1991)

What Is a Family? by Gretchen Super (Troll Associates, 1991)

Tooth Tally

Graph Question: *How many teeth have you lost?*

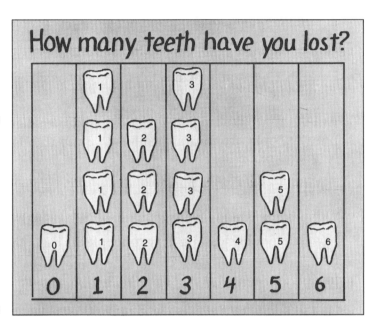

How many teeth have you lost?

0   1   2   3   4   5   6

About the Lesson ••••

Toothless grins are common among primary children. Here's one way to capitalize on students' fascination with their wiggly teeth. You may want to relate this graph to a lesson on tooth care.

Making the Graph ••••

1. Prepare the graph surface by making a grid pattern on the tag board. Boxes on the grid should be large enough to accommodate the tooth patterns on page 28. Label the base of each vertical column with the numbers 0 to 10.

2. Ask children how many, if any, of their baby teeth have fallen out. Distribute a tooth pattern to each child. Ask children to write the number of teeth they have lost on their tooth pattern. If they have not lost any teeth yet, they can write the number "0" on the pattern.

3. Call students to the graph in groups by asking questions about the number of teeth they have lost: "How many people have lost one tooth?"; "How many have lost two teeth?" and so on. Have children glue their tooth pattern in the appropriate column on the graph.

Materials
- Tooth patterns (see reproducible page 28)
- Piece of colored tag board
- Markers
- Glue

4. Once children have graphed the information, ask volunteers to total each column. Children can write the totals on extra tooth patterns and glue the numbers to the top of each column.

Reading the Graph ••••••••••••••

- Has everybody lost at least one tooth? If not, how many people have not lost any teeth?

- What is the greatest number of teeth that anyone has lost?

- Have more people lost one tooth or three teeth?

- Count the number of people who have lost two teeth. What is the total number of teeth lost by this group? (Hint: Count by two's.)

- What is the total number of teeth our class has lost?

Teaching Tip

Tell children that chewing food is the first step in digesting it. To help students see the different ways teeth begin digesting foods, have them sample a variety of snacks such as apples, celery, lettuce, nuts, raisins, pudding, cheese cubes, fruit leather, peanut butter, and gelatin. Ask children to pay attention to the various chewing styles (ripping, tearing, and grinding) they employ for each one.

Variation •••••••••••••••••••••••••••••••••••••••

Pass out hand mirrors to children and have them do a tooth count. Students can then create a graph showing how many teeth they have in their mouth.

Supporting Literature

How Many Teeth? by Paul Showers (HarperCollins, 1991)

When I See My Dentist by Susan Kuklin (Bradbury Press, 1988)

Tooth Patterns

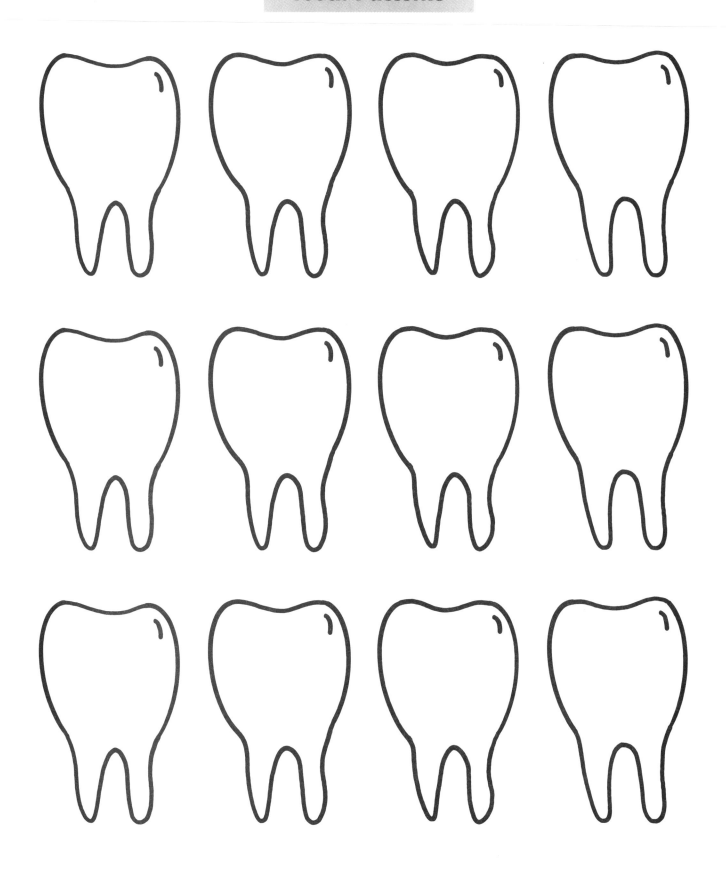

You Can Count on Wheels

Graph Question: *How many wheels do different vehicles have?*

About the Lesson

Our kindergarten and first-grade classes made this graph for a school-wide math fair. Children first generated a list of vehicles. They then went on to classify these vehicles according to the number of wheels they have. Naturally, this activity lends itself well to a unit on transportation.

Materials

- 5-by-7-inch unlined index cards (or vehicle patterns on reproducible pages 31 and 32)
- Crayons or markers
- Colored construction paper
- Scissors
- Large sheet of mural paper
- Glue

Making the Graph

1. Brainstorm and record a list of vehicles that have wheels. Ask children to compare the number of wheels that the different vehicles have.

2. Distribute one index card to each student. Ask children to draw on the card one of the vehicles from your list. Then have them label each card with the name of the vehicle. (To save time, you can use the vehicle patterns on pages 31 and 32.)

3. In large block or bubble writing, draw the numerals 1 to 6, 8, 12, and 18 on colored paper to represent the number of wheels on different vehicles. Cut the numerals out.

4. Lay out the mural paper. Draw a grid on the paper to create the graphing surface. The boxes should be wide enough to accommodate the index cards. Tape the numerals onto the left-hand side of the paper in a single column, keeping them in numerical order.

5. Invite children to gather around the graph with their vehicle cards. Ask each child to state the number of wheels on his or her vehicle. Students can then glue their cards on the graph in the row specifying the number of wheels that their vehicle has.

Reading the Graph •••••••

- How many vehicles had two wheels? *(substitute other numbers)*

- How many wheels did most of our vehicles have?

- Which vehicles had the least number of wheels?

- Do all vehicles have an even number of wheels?

- Why do some vehicles have more wheels than others?

Teaching Tip

Use the information on the graph in some problem solving activities. For example, ask: If 10 wheels are on the road, what combination of vehicles is possible? (i.e., unicycle + wheelbarrow + car + van = 10 wheels). When we tried this activity, each kindergartner worked with a first-grade buddy to draw the illustrations needed to solve the problem. The vehicles were identified and an equation was noted. The pictures were mounted and bound together to form an accordion-style book entitled "You Can Count on Wheels."

Variations ••••••••••••••••••••••••••••••••••••••

- Have children draw land, sea, and air vehicles (or use those pictured on reproducible pages 31 and 32). Graph the vehicles according to these criteria.

- Create a graph showing the different ways children get to school: by foot, by bus, by car, by skates, and so on.

Supporting Literature

Big Wheels by Anne Rockwell (Trumpet Club, 1986)

Trains by Byron Barton (Trumpet Club, 1986)

Flying by Donald Crews (Scholastic Inc., 1986)

Trains by Gail Gibbons (Scholastic Inc., 1987)

Vehicle Patterns

Vehicle Patterns

One Potato More

Graphing Question: *How do you like to eat potatoes?*

About the Lesson

During a unit on food, we asked each child to bring a potato to class. The potatoes were used in art and science lessons. These activities led to the making of a potato graph on which children recorded their favorite ways to eat this popular food.

Making the Graph

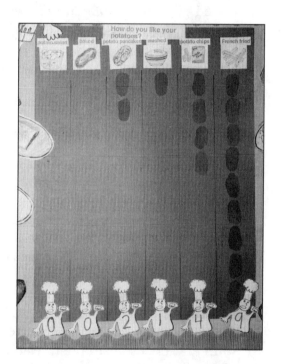

1. Begin a discussion about the different ways in which potatoes can be prepared, such as, baked, french fried, potato salad, potato chips, potato pancakes, etc. Be sure to include preparation methods from a variety of cultures.

2. Create a column on the tag board for each of the potato dishes mentioned in your discussion.

3. Ask volunteers to draw pictures of the potato dishes. Glue these to the top of the tag board to serve as picture-labels for each column.

4. Cut potato shapes from brown construction paper (or use the pattern on page 35). Distribute a potato shape to each child.

5. Allow each child to tape/glue a potato shape onto the graph in the column that shows his or her favorite way to eat potatoes. Total the columns.

Materials

- Large piece of tag board
- Brown construction paper (or food pattern from reproducible page 35)
- Scissors
- Markers
- Tape/glue

Reading the Graph ·············

- How many different ways do students in our class like to eat potatoes?

- How many children like to eat their potatoes hot? (baked, fried, mashed, etc.)

- How many children like their potatoes cold? (potato salad, potato chips, etc.)

- What kind of potato dish is enjoyed by the most children?

- How many more children like french fries than baked potatoes? *(substitute other potato dishes)*

- Is the number of children who like potato pancakes greater or less than the number of children who like potato dumplings? *(substitute other potato dishes)*

Variations ·····················

- This graph can be adapted for use with a variety of other foods. Read *Everybody Cooks Rice* by Norah Dooley (Carolrhoda, 1991) or *Bread Bread Bread* by Ann Morris (Lothrop, 1989). Create graphs focusing on the different varieties of these staple foods. Other ideas for food graphs: How do children like to eat corn? (on the cob, off the cob, as popcorn, in corn bread, as corn chips or corn flakes, etc.) What's their favorite sandwich? (peanut butter and jelly, ham and cheese, tuna fish, egg salad, etc.) How about their favorite pasta dish? (spaghetti, ravioli, macaroni and cheese, lo mein, noodle kugel, etc.) (See page 35 for food patterns to use in graphing.)

- Have children measure and weigh real potatoes and create a graph comparing their lengths or weights.

(See page 35 for food patterns to use in graphing.)

Teaching Tips

- Use this graph as an opportunity to talk about nutrition. Ask: Are some preparation methods healthier than others (i.e., baked potatoes vs. potato chips)? Why or why not? Are our favorite ways to eat potatoes the healthiest choices?

- To add a writing component to this graphing activity, invite children to create recipes for the potato dishes they included on the graph. Before they begin, discuss the key parts of a recipe: ingredients, cooking directions, time, and temperature. You may want to try this as a take-home activity, asking students' families to share recipes for their favorite potato dishes. Compile the recipes to make a potato cookbook, complete with illustrations. Try out some of the simpler recipes in class.

Supporting Literature

One Potato by Sue Porter (The Trumpet Club, 1989)

One Potato, Two Potato, Three Potato, Four compiled by Mary Lou Colgin (Gryphon House, 1982)

Rice

Pleasant Dreams

Graph Question: *What time do you go to bed at night?*

About the Lesson ·······

As part of a unit on the theme of Day and Night, our class read stories about bedtime. This led naturally to a discussion about the bedtimes of children in the class. Students made cutout clocks to show their bedtimes, then graphed them for comparison. Since students had just learned to tell time, this graph offered an excellent opportunity to practice their newly developed skill.

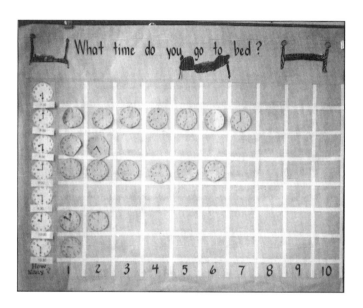

Materials

- Colored craft paper
- Colored masking tape
- Clock stamp
- Clock pattern (see reproducible page 38)
- Scissors
- Markers
- Glue

Making the Graph ················

1. Cover a bulletin board with the colored paper.

2. Use colored masking tape to create a grid pattern on the graph surface. Boxes on the grid should be large enough to accommodate the clock pattern on page 38.

3. Write the numbers 1 to 10 in a row along the bottom of the graph. This will help children tally the information on the graph later.

4. Use the clock stamp to prepare possible student bedtimes. Place one clock at the beginning of each row on the graph. For our graph, clocks were marked on the hour and half hour (7:00, 7:30, 8:00). Write the time in numbers under each clock pattern to help children read the time.

5. Provide each child with a copy of the clock pattern on page 38. Ask children to draw hands on the clock to show the time they go to bed at night. Have them cut out the clock patterns.

6. Invite students to approach the graph one by one and glue the clock pattern in the appropriate row. Tell children they can find the correct row by matching the position of the hands on their clock with the position of the hands on one of the clocks on the graph. Have children say their bedtime aloud as they glue their clock in place on the graph.

Reading the Graph ••••••••••••••

- How many children go to bed at 8:00? *(substitute other times)*

- What is the earliest bedtime?

- What is the latest bedtime?

- How many children go to bed before 8:30?

- How many children go to bed after 9:00?

- What time do most children go to bed?

Teaching Tip

If the graphing clocks are marked on the hour and the half hour, what do you do if a child reports a bedtime of 8:15? You can either adjust the clocks on the graphing surface or round off the times to the nearest hour or half hour.

Variations ••••••••••••••••••••••••••••••••

Suggest that children graph the time they get up in the morning, the time they eat dinner, or the time they go to bed on weekends (as opposed to school nights).

Supporting Literature

The Napping House by Audrey Wood (Harcourt, Brace, Jovanovich, 1984)

Time To.... by Bruce McMillan (Scholastic Inc., 1989)

Clock Patterns

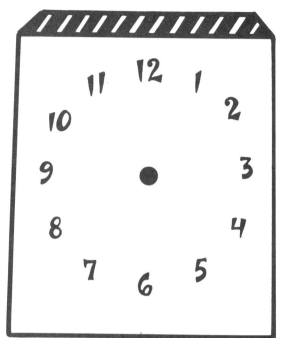

Chapter Three

Symbol Graphs

These graphs involve the use of symbols (check marks, stickers, tally marks) to indicate information on a graph.

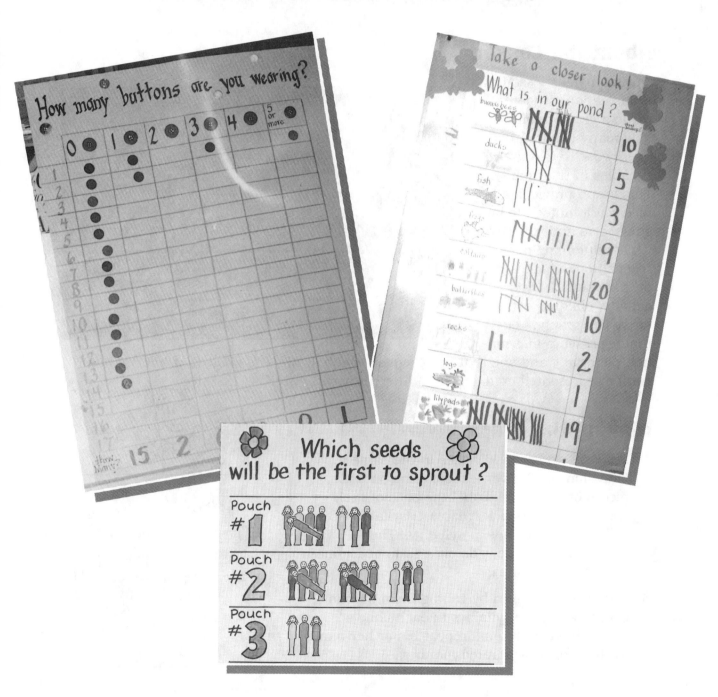

Parts of a Name

Graph Question: *How many syllables are in your first name?*

About the Lesson

During a skills lesson on syllabication, students made a graph to show how many children had one, two, three, or more syllables in their name. This graph provides a nice way to integrate language arts and math while reinforcing name recognition, which is a primary skill. In this activity, children will make two graphs—one that represents information pictorially and one that represents it symbolically—to show that information can be represented on a graph in different ways.

Making the Graph

1. Prepare two graph surfaces in the same way. Draw four or five vertical columns on both pieces of tag board. Label the base of each column as follows: 1 syllable, 2 syllables, 3 syllables, 4 syllables, 5 syllables. The columns should be wide enough to accommodate the paper slips.

2. Gather the children by calling them by name, exaggerating the syllables in each child's name. Have each child repeat his or her name in the same exaggerated manner.

Materials

- 2 pieces of tag board
- Markers
- Paper strips (approximately 1 by 3 inches)
- Scissors
- Glue

3. Explain to students that each part of their name is a syllable. Ask children to tell you how many syllables they hear in their names.

4. Provide each student with a paper strip and have the child record his or her name on it. Tell children to cut the paper strip into pieces to reflect the syllable breaks in their names.

5. Display one of the tag board graph surfaces. Ask children to glue the segments of their name strips in the column that reflects the number of syllables in their name. Tally the number of names in each column.

6. Place the second piece of tag board next to the first. Show students how to use a symbol, such as a check mark, to stand for their names. Enlist their help in transferring the information from the first graph onto the second graph. Allow time for children to compare and discuss the two graphs.

Reading the Graph ••••••••••••••

- Which names contained the greatest number of syllables? The smallest number?

- What can you say about the names of the children in our class—are they long or short?

- Do you think this is the way it is in other classes?

- If my name was Esperenza, in which column would I write my name? *(substitute various names)*

- Can you think of other names for the 2-syllable column? Can you think of any for the 5-syllable column?

- How are the two graphs we made similar? How are they different? What are the advantages of each?

- How is using symbols to represent information helpful? What other symbols could we use on a graph?

> ### Teaching Tip
>
> The use of musical instruments will enhance the study of syllables. Have the children say their names while playing percussion or string instruments for a musical accompaniment to this activity.

Variations •••••••••••••••••••••••••••••••••••

- Children can graph the number of letters, instead of syllables, in their first name or last name.

- Look for syllabication in other names and create similar graphs. Some topics to try: dinosaur names, plant names, state names, presidents' names.

Buttons Galore

Graph Question: *How many buttons are you wearing?*

About the Lesson •••••

Buttons are a familiar manipulative in the primary classroom. They can be used to introduce the concepts of sorting and classifying, which lead naturally to graphing. This simple graph served as an introduction to our work with buttons.

Materials

- Tag board
- Markers
- Stickers

Making the Graph ••••••••••••••••••••••••••••

1. Use a marker to divide the tag board into five or six vertical columns. Label the columns as follows: 0 buttons, 1 button, 2 buttons, 3 buttons, 4 buttons, 5 or more buttons. Draw horizontal lines across the columns to create a grid pattern.

2. Ask students to count the number of buttons found on their clothing.

3. Provide each student with a sticker. Have children come up to the graph one by one and place a sticker in the space under the column that shows their button count.

Reading the Graph •••••••••••••••

- Are more children wearing buttons or not wearing buttons today?

- Do the results of our graph surprise you?

- How many children are wearing two buttons? How many are wearing four buttons? *(substitute other numbers from the graph)*

- Are more children wearing three buttons or five buttons? Zero buttons or one button? *(substitute other numbers from the graph)*

Variations ••••••••••••••••••••••

- Try this activity as an object graph using actual buttons instead of stickers. Buttons can be purchased commercially, or you may want to start a button collection as a class project. Have the students bring home a letter requesting buttons of various shapes, sizes, and colors. Ask for help from local tailors, fabric stores, or craft shops. Challenge children to come up with different ways to sort your button collection. Create graphs that reflect these various groupings.

- Alternatively, have children color in the button patterns on reproducible page 44. They can cut out the button patterns and use them to create a picture graph instead of an object graph.

Teaching Tips

- Glue sets of buttons onto index cards. Create several cards with different numbers of buttons: one button, two buttons, three buttons, and so on. Divide the class into small groups. Refer students back to the button graph you created. Ask the groups to calculate the total number of buttons represented in each column of the graph. (For example, if there are four stickers in the "4-button" column, the total number of buttons is 16.) Allow the groups to use the button cards you prepared as counting manipulatives to help them with the calculations. Challege children to determine the total number of buttons worn by your class that day.

- Redo the graph on the following day to see how the results differ. Or invite another class to try the same activity and compare the findings.

Supporting Literature

The Button Box by Margarette Reid (Dutton, 1990)

Corduroy by Don Freeman (Scholastic, 1968)

"The Lost Button" from *Frog and Toad Are Friends* by Arnold Lobel (Scholastic Inc., 1970)

Button Patterns

Who's in Our Habitat?

Graph Question: *What do you see in the pond?*

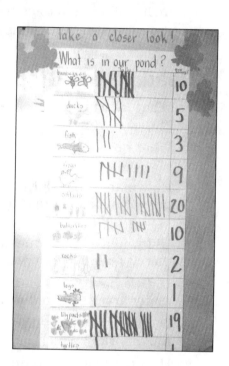

About the Lesson

In this activity, children use tally marks to group and count items they've included on a habitat mural. We used a pond environment for the basis of our graph, but the same idea can be applied to many different murals created in the primary classroom. This activity will help you integrate art, science, and math into one lesson.

Making the Graph

1. After your class has finished making the mural, discuss the numerous and varied items found on it. Solicit ideas from children about how you might create a graph to show what's included on the mural.

Materials

- Mural (based on a theme covered in your class)
- Chart paper
- File cards
- Crayons
- Large sheet of white art paper
- Tape/glue
- Markers

2. Ask children to itemize what's on the mural. Record this information on the chalk board or chart paper.

3. Label a file card with the name of each item you recorded. Ask students to illustrate each labeled card.

4. Mount the file cards on the art paper. Place the cards in a vertical column on the left-hand side of the paper. To complete the graph surface, separate the file cards with horizontal lines that extend to the right edge of the paper.

5. Decide which item on the mural to begin counting and count all of the items in that group. For our pond mural and graph, we began by counting frogs.

6. Select a child to come to the graph to serve as a recorder. As you or a student points to an item on the mural, the recorder should make a tally mark next to the appropriate file card.

7. Once all the items on the mural are recorded, invite volunteers to come up and total each group, writing the totals at the end of each row.

Reading the Graph ••••••••••••

- What information can be learned from our pond graph?

- What does our pond have the most of? The least of?

- How many frogs did we have? How many tadpoles? *(substitute appropriate categories from your graph)*

- Did we have more ducks or fish? How many more? *(substitute appropriate categories)*

- Did we have fewer cattails or lily pads? How many fewer? *(substitute appropriate categories)*

- Did any two items have the same number of tally marks? Which ones?

- How many items on our graph are living? How many are nonliving?

Teaching Tip

Before you begin this activity, review with children how to record information and count with tally marks. Show them how the fifth line is drawn diagonally across the first four lines to make a set of five. Ask children how this method of recording information can help people count *(it's quicker to count by fives)*. Expose children to the use of tally marks in everyday activities, such as taking attendance and taking a lunch count. Encourage children to use the tally marks to count by fives to practice this math skill.

Variation •••••••••••••••••••••••••••••••••••••••

Habitat murals lend themselves particularly well to this type of graphing activity. Try creating a mural and graph based on the following themes: deciduous forest, rain forest, ocean, desert, the Arctic. Other suggestions for murals on which to base graphs: On the Farm, At the Zoo, In the Garden, City Life, and so on.

Supporting Literature

Puddles and Ponds by Rose Wyler (Silver Burdett, 1990)

Pond Life by Donna Koren Wells (Childrens Press, 1990)

Ready, Set, Sprout!

Graph Question: *Which seeds will be the first to sprout?*

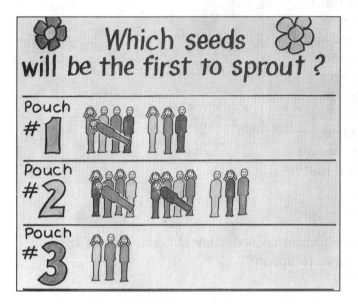

About the Lesson ·········

Graphing and science go hand in hand. Students can use graphs to predict outcomes, record their observations, and compare the results in different experiments. In this activity, children create a tally graph to record their predictions about which seeds will be the first to sprout in a plant-growth experiment.

Making the Graph ··········

1. Set up a simple experiment in which children test the best conditions for sprouting seeds. Seek children's input as you come up with different variables to test.

2. Prepare seed pouches that reflect the different conditions you have decided to test. For example, you may want to investigate how light and air affect seeds' ability to sprout. To prepare the pouches, wet four paper towels, scatter a few seeds on each, and put them in separate plastic bags. Leave two bags unsealed and tape one to a sunny window and one bag inside a dark closet.

Materials

- Fast-sprouting seeds such as mung bean, radish, or alfalfa
- Paper towels
- Water
- Self-sealing plastic bags
- Masking tape
- Markers
- Tag board
- People tally patterns (optional; see reproducible page 50)

Squeeze excess air out of the other two bags and seal them shut. Tape one of these bags on the window and one in the closet. Use the masking tape to label each seed pouch: #1, #2, #3, and #4.

3. Use a marker to divide the tag board into four rows. Label each row with one of the seed pouch numbers.

4. Ask children to predict which seed pouch they think will sprout first. Invite children to approach the graph surface one by one and write a tally mark in the row that reflects their prediction. (Remind any child making the fifth mark to draw it across the others diagonally.) As students draw their tally marks, encourage them to explain their predictions. For a cute way to record student responses, use the cutout people patterns on reproducible page 50. They can be used just like tally marks.

Teaching Tip

Making predictions is an important part of the scientific process. You can use graphs to record students' predictions in a range of science experiments. Encourage children to relate their predictions to the results of each experiment.

5. Ask volunteers to total each row of the graph.

6. Over the next week or so, suggest that children record their observations of the seeds in each pouch as they wait for them to sprout.

Reading the Graph •••••••••••••••••••••••••••••••••••••

- How many predicted that seed pouch #1 would sprout first?
- How many predicted seed pouch #3 would be first?
- Did more think seed pouch #2 or seed pouch #4 would sprout first?
- How many children guessed correctly about which pouch would sprout first?
- Were there more children who guessed correctly or incorrectly? How many more?
- What did we learn about the conditions needed for seeds to sprout?

Variations •••

- Instead of making predictions about the optimal conditions for growth, have children graph their predictions about how long it will take seeds in one pouch to sprout: one day? two days? three days? and so on.
- Tally graphs can also be used for recording predictions in reading activities.

When reading a story, pause at appropriate points and ask children to predict what they think will happen next or to predict the ending. Create a quick tally graph on the chalkboard.

- Use tally graphs for "quick counts" that answer simple yes or no questions, or to conduct a simple survey. Some suggestions for "quick count" graphs: Can you tie your shoes? Can you write your name? Do you have a pet? Who is your favorite author? Which do you like better, apples or oranges? and so on. Ask children to suggest fun ways to display the information. For example, you might create a shoe pattern on which to record information about who can tie their shoes, or an apple and an orange for the fruit comparison.

Supporting Literature

The Carrot Seed by Ruth Krauss (HarperCollins, 1945)

From Seed to Plant by Gail Gibbons (Holiday House, 1991)

Kids Gardening: A Kids' Guide to Messing Around in the Dirt by Kevin Rafferty (Klutz Press, 1989)

People Tally Pattern

Chapter Four

Venn Diagrams

This graphic form uses two or more overlapping circles to organize information and highlight shared characteristics.

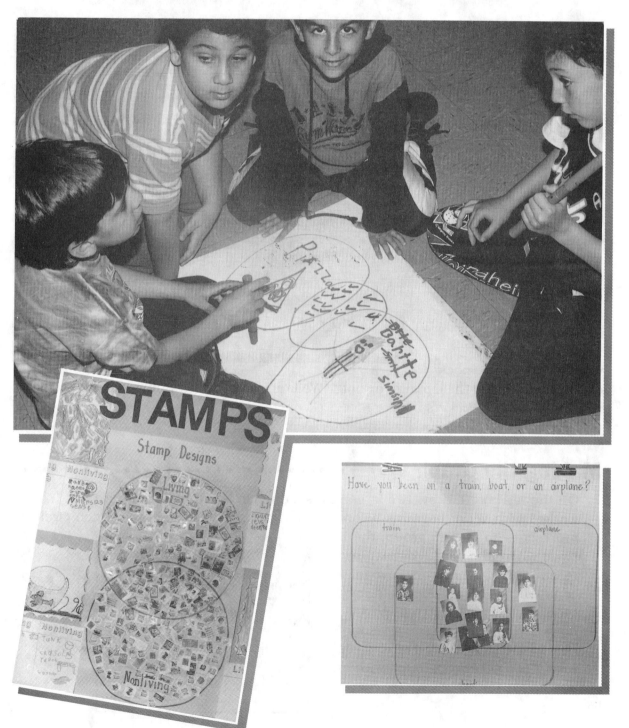

Plenty of Pockets

Graph Question: *Where are your pockets?*

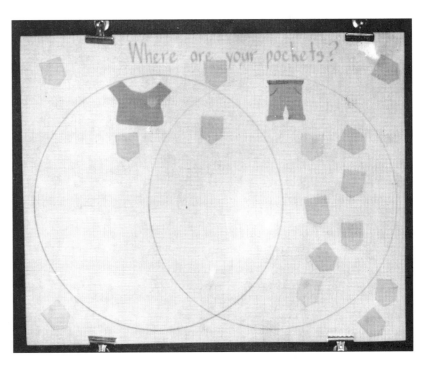

About the Lesson ·········

Venn diagrams are an excellent way for children to visualize the similarities and differences between two or more things. This simple graphing activity provides a good introduction to the format. In it, children record information about whether they have pockets on their shirts, their pants, or both. We launched this graphing activity with a reading of *Peter's Pockets* by Eve Rice.

Making the Graph ·······························

1. On the tag board, draw two large intersecting circles. If children have not worked with Venn diagrams before, explain the parts of the graph: Each circle represents a different group; the place where the circles overlap represents what the groups have in common. It's a good idea to draw each circle with a different color marker. This will provide a visual clue to the fact that the circles represent two separate groups with one shared area.

Materials

- Tag board
- Markers
- Shirt, pants, and pockets patterns (see reproducible page 55)
- Glue

2. Glue the shirt pattern above one circle and the pants pattern above the other to label the parts of the graph.

3. Tell children you are going to use these circles to organize information about who has pockets on their clothing and where the pockets are. Ask children to look at their clothing to see whether or not they have pockets.

4. Discuss where students found pockets on their clothing, if at all. Do they have shirt pockets only, pants pockets only, or both? Where would they note this information on the graph? Ask students where on the graph they could note those people who don't have any pockets (outside the circles).

5. Distribute a pocket pattern to each child. Ask children to approach the graph one by one and glue the pattern on the part that shows where they have pockets.

Reading the Graph ••••••••••••

- How many children have pockets on their shirts? How many have pockets on their pants?

- What information does the place where the two circles meet tell us? How many children belong to this group?

- How many children don't have any pockets?

- Are there more children with pockets or without pockets?

- Do more children have pockets on their shirts only, their pants only, or on both their shirts and pants?

Teaching Tip

Since wearing sweatpants and sweatshirts to school has become more popular, be prepared for the fact that many children may not have any pockets. Discuss how the number of pockets changes depending on the style of clothing worn to school. Also, if girls have pockets on their skirts, explain that they can include these in the "pants pocket" group.

Variations •••

- A kinesthetic activity can help children understand the conceptual basis of a Venn diagram. Take children outside to the playground or to another open area. Use chalk to draw two very large intersecting circles. Be sure there's plenty of room in the middle where the circles overlap. Now ask children to recreate the pocket graph they made in the classroom. Those children with pockets on their shirts can stand in one circle, those with pockets on their pants in another, and children with pockets in both places can stand in the place where the two circles intersect. Students without pockets can stand outside the circles. Have children count off to tally the groupings.

- Use the pocket patterns to create a picture graph showing the number of pockets children have on their clothing. Each child can write his or her total number of pockets on a pattern, then group their patterns into different columns to form the picture graph. Students may want to include the number of pockets on their jackets and bookbags in the pocket count, too. (See pages 10 to 12 for more graphing ideas related to the theme of clothing.)

Supporting Literature

Peter's Pockets by Eve Rice (Greenwillow Books, 1989)

A Pocket for Corduroy by Don Freeman (Scholastic Inc., 1978)

Katy No-Pocket by Emmy Payne (Houghton Mifflin Co., 1944)

There's a Hole in My Pocket adapted by Akimi Gibson (Scholastic, 1994)

Pocket Patterns

Stuck on Stamps

Graph Question: *What kinds of pictures do we see on stamps?*

About the Lesson ··········

Stamps are a great manipulative to use in graphing activities. Following a lesson on the postal system, children in our class were given two weeks to collect stamps. After a class discussion, we found that the entire collection could be grouped on a Venn diagram under the categories of "Living" and "Nonliving," with stamps that pictured both things falling in the overlapping area.

Materials

- Large sheet of butcher paper
- Markers
- Student graphing sheet (see reproducible page 58)
- Stamps
- Glue
- Glue brush

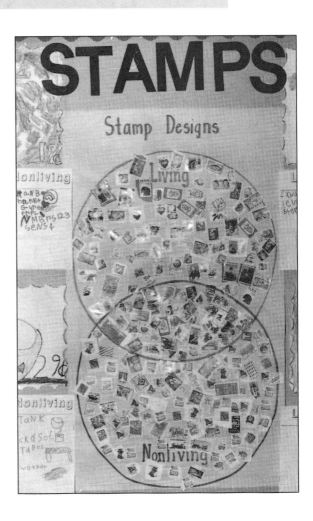

Making the Graph ·····························

1. Provide examples of living and nonliving things and discuss the properties of each. Continue the discussion by having children search the classroom for living and nonliving things.

2. Prepare the graphing surface by drawing two large, overlapping circles on the butcher paper. Label one "Living" and one "Nonliving."

3. Tell students that they are going to look at stamps to see if they picture living or nonliving things. Show children examples of stamps that could be included in these categories. Ask children to point out where the stamps might be placed on the graphing surface.

4. Ask students to offer ideas about what might go in the part of the graph where the two circles overlap. Once students have identified that this area can be used to show stamps that depict both living and nonliving things, ask them to provide an example, such as a stamp showing a man standing in front of a building.

5. Distribute a copy of the student graphing sheet and a handful of stamps to each child. Model grouping the stamps.

6. Direct the children to use their student graphing sheets to sort their stamps by placing them (not gluing them) on the appropriate parts of the Venn diagram. Encourage interaction among the children while they are working.

7. When the students finish grouping the stamps, combine their work on the class graph. Use a glue brush to spread glue over a large portion of the "Living" section of the Venn diagram. Call a few children at a time to place the stamps from the "Living" group on their own graphs on the class graph. Repeat the process with the "Nonliving" group and the combined group.

Teaching Tip

Try this activity during the holiday season; students will be able to collect a greater variety and number of stamps. Decorate and set aside a special box in which students can store stamps that they collect throughout the year.

Reading the Graph • • • • • • • • • • • • • •

• Which group seems to have the most stamps? How can we find out if we are correct?

• Do more stamps show living things or nonliving things? How many more?

• Are there less stamps showing living and nonliving things combined, or less showing just living things? How many less?

• If I found a stamp that had a sunflower on it, where would it go on the Venn diagram? How about a stamp showing a teddy bear?

Variation •

• Ask students to suggest different ways you might group stamps, for example, by country of origin, value, shape (squares vs. rectangles), or theme (space, animals, famous people, plants). Graph stamps according to these criteria.

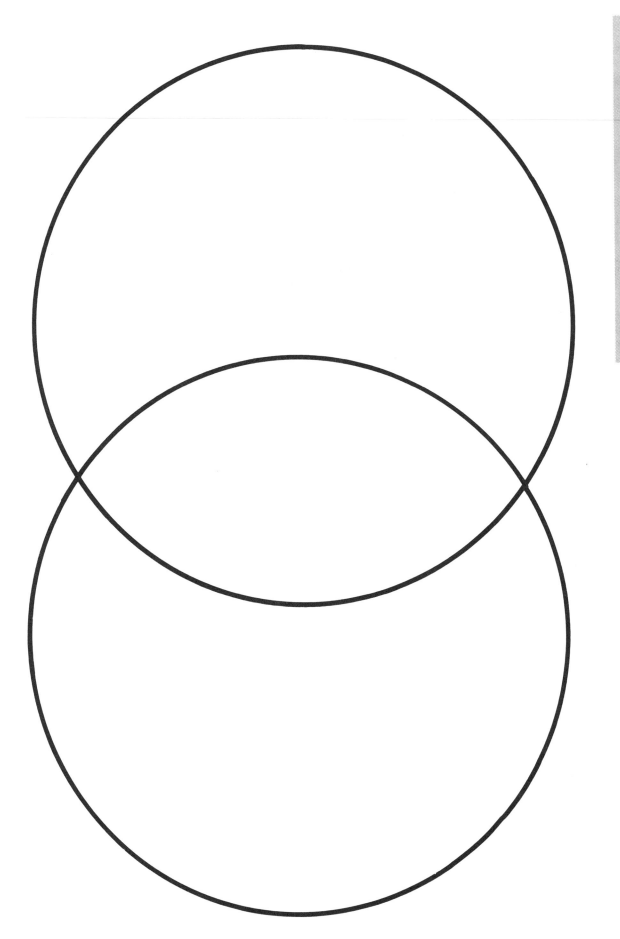

Name _____

Along for the Ride

Graph Question: *Have you been on a train or an airplane?*

About the Lesson

Here's another graph to use during a unit on transportation. For this activity, children pasted photos of themselves on a Venn diagram to answer the graph question.

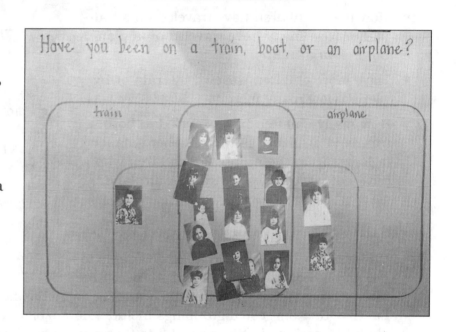

Making the Graph

1. Through literature and discussion, explore various means of transportation. What types of transportation have children traveled on? Ask volunteers to talk about their experiences. Tell children you're going to take a class poll about who has traveled on two different types of transportation, and graph the results. Our class decided to compare travel on trains and airplanes.

2. Draw two intersecting forms on the tag board (circles, squares, or rectangles). Color the train and plane patterns and use them to label each part of the graph. Discuss what the middle part of the graph represents in relation to the graph question (people who have traveled on both trains and planes).

Materials

- Tag board
- Markers
- Glue stick
- Airplane and train patterns
- A picture of each child (photocopied from school photos)

3. Make sure each child has a picture of him- or herself. Ask children to answer the graph question by placing their photos in one of the three sections of the graph. If they have not traveled on either a plane or a train, children should tape their photos in the area outside the intersecting forms.

Reading the Graph

- How many children have traveled on a train? How many children have traveled on a train, *but not* on an airplane?

- How many children have traveled on an airplane? How many have traveled on a plane, *but not* on a train?

- Have more children traveled by train or by plane? How many more?

- How many children have traveled in both a train and airplane? Is this number smaller or larger than the number of children who have not yet traveled by train or airplane?

Teaching Tip

It's great to have photocopies of children's school pictures on hand. These can be used in many different graphing formats to indicate which group a child falls into, or to register a child's vote in a class survey. The photos give children an immediate connection with the information on a graph.

Variations

- Children may want to add a third variable to the graph. For example, they might use three intersecting circles to answer the question, "Who has been on a train, plane, or boat?" Other suggested groupings include: horse/bicycle/car, rollerskates/in-line skates/skateboard. (See pages 63 to 65 for more on Venn diagrams involving three intersecting circles; see pages 29 and 30 for more graphing activities related to the theme of transportation.)

- Create Venn diagrams to compare other experiences students have had, for example, places they have visited, foods they have tasted, or books they have read.

- For a nice partner sharing activity, divide the class into pairs and provide each with a copy of the Venn diagram pattern on page 58. Ask children to use the pattern to show the ways they are similar to and different from one another (heritage, families, hobbies, likes and dislikes, and so on).

Supporting Literature

See page 30 for suggested books on transportation.

Lost Mittens

Graph Question: *How do different versions of the same folktale compare with one another?*

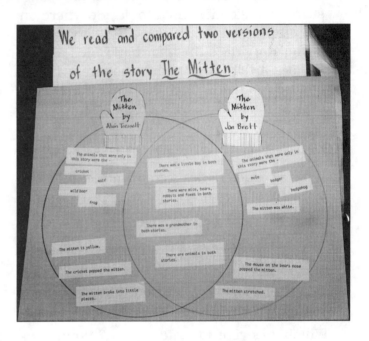

About the Lesson

We often use Venn diagrams for book comparisons. Graphs are a great way to get students to pay close attention to detail in a story. They're also a good tool for assessing comprehension. The purpose of the Venn diagram in this activity was to compare two versions of the folktale *The Mitten*, but you can use any folktale or fairy tale with multiple versions.

Making the Graph

1. Read both versions of the story. Ask students to point out some of the narrative details in the story (i.e., the color of the mitten, animals appearing in the story, what happened to the mitten at the end of the story) as you read each of the books. Record this information on chart paper.

2. Rewrite students' ideas on small strips of paper (or type the information on a word processor and cut the printout into strips).

Materials

- *The Mitten* by Jan Brett (Scholastic Inc., 1989)
- *The Mitten* by Alvin Tresselt (Scholastic Inc., 1964)
- Chart paper
- Small strips of paper
- Tag board
- Marker
- Tape or glue

3. Prepare the graph surface by drawing two intersecting circles on the tag board. Label each circle with the title and author of one version of *The Mitten*. Tell children you are going to use these circles to compare the two stories. Review the parts of the graph with children: The left circle represents one version of the story, the right circle the other, and the place where they overlap represents what they have in common.

4. Have children gather together in front of the graph. Provide each child with one of the paper strips which you used to record information from the books. Reread the information on each strip and ask each child to decide where on the graph the strip belongs. Which version of the story does the information tell about, or does it tell about both? Encourage the children to justify their responses as they tape or glue their strips on the graph.

Reading the Graph ••••••••••••

- What characteristics were common to both versions of the story?

- What characteristics applied only to Alvin Tresselt's book?

- What characteristics applied only to Jan Brett's book?

- Based on the graph, do you think the stories were more alike than different, or more different than alike?

- Which was your favorite version? Why? What did you like about it that wasn't in the other version?

Teaching Tip

A reenactment of the stories will help the children better understand and remember the details. The teacher may also help the children by supporting the printed statements on the graph with pictures. This will be particularly helpful for nonreaders.

Variation ••••••••••••••••••••••••••••••••••••

Many folktales and fairy tales are told all over the world. Examining different versions of the same tale is a good way to explore diverse cultures and to help children see similarities and differences among the world's peoples. Here are two more suggestions for tales to compare using a Venn diagram.

- "The Three Little Pigs":
  The Three Little Pigs by Paul Galdone (Scholastic Inc., 1970)
  The Three Little Javelinas by Susan Lowell (Scholastic Inc., 1992)
  The Three Little Pigs by James Marshall (Scholastic Inc., 1989)

- "Little Red Riding Hood":
  Little Red Riding Hood by Karen Schmidt (Scholastic Inc., 1986)
  Lon Po Po by Ed Young (Scholastic Inc., 1989)
  Red Riding Hood by James Marshall (Scholastic Inc., 1987)

A Cunning Character

Graph Question: *What characteristics does a fictional fox share with a real fox? With humans?*

About the Lesson

Here's another suggestion for using Venn diagrams to enhance literature studies. This activity also integrates science as children compare a real animal with a fictional animal. There are lots of books about animals that lend themselves to this graphing experience. We used James Marshall's series of *Fox* books because young children easily

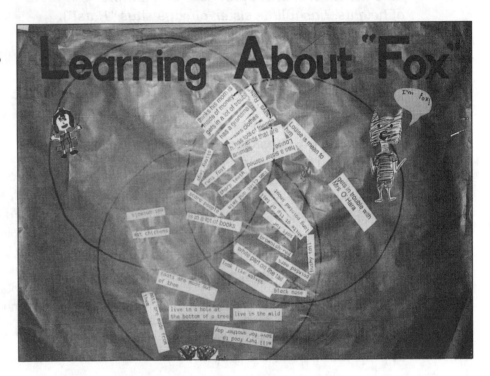

identify with the character. Our class also read nonfiction books about foxes. Books can be read aloud by the teacher or independently by fluent readers. This graph works well as a bulletin board display.

Materials

- Art paper
- Writing paper
- Marker
- Some of the books in James Marshall's Fox" series (all published by Dial Books): *Fox Outfoxed, Fox on the Job, Fox All Week, Fox Be Nimble, Fox and His Friends, Fox on Stage, Fox at School, Fox in Love*
- Glue

Making the Graph ••••••••••••••••••••••••••••••••••••••

1. Cover a bulletin board with art paper. Draw three large intersecting circles. Make sure the spaces where the circles intersect are roomy, since Fox shares many characteristics both with real foxes and with humans.

2. Photocopy pictures of the character Fox, a real fox, and a person. Glue one picture in each circle to label the parts of the graph.

3. While reading the *Fox* books, keep a growing list of the title character's appearance, behavior, friends, expressions, and other characteristics. This list should take the form of short phrases (for example, *is afraid of heights, has a little sister, always says "Rats!"*).

4. After you have finished reading the books, cut apart the list of phrases to make small strips. Mix up the strips and distribute one or more to each child.

5. Review the different parts of the graph. Ask children how many categories there are on the graphing surface (seven). Have them try to identify all of them. You may want to prompt children with questions such as, "Which part of the graph shows what Fox has in common with people? Which part shows what Fox has in common with real foxes? Which part shows what Fox has in common with real foxes *and* with people?"

6. Have each child read his or her strip and explain where it should be placed on the Venn diagram. Guide children as they place their strips on the appropriate part of the graph.

Teaching Tip

Since this graph compares three different things (a real fox, a fictional fox, and a human being), it is a bit more challenging than the preceding activities. Try it only after children have had some experience with the two-circle Venn diagram format.

Reading the Graph ••••••••••••••••••••••••••••••••••••••

- Name two ways Fox is different from real foxes. Name two ways he is like them.

- Does Fox share many characteristics with humans? What are some of these characteristics?

- Based on the information on the graph, does the character Fox have more in common with real foxes or with people?

- Are there any ways in which Fox, real foxes, and humans are alike? What are they?

- What other things does the graph tell us about Fox?

Variations •

- Compare other fictional animals with their real-life counterparts. Some animal characters to try include:

  1. Turtles: *Franklin in the Dark* by Paulette Bourgeois (Scholastic Inc., 1986) and other Franklin stories.

  2. Monkeys: *Curious George* by H.A. Rey (HarperCollins, 1941) and other *Curious George* stories.

  3. Spiders: *Charlotte's Web* by E.B. White (HarperCollins, 1952)

  4. Mice: *Frederick* by Leo Lionni (Pantheon, 1963)

- Venn diagrams are also a great way to compare two characters in the same story. Try comparing James Marshall's George and Martha characters, Arnold Lobel's Frog and Toad characters, or the Country Mouse and the City Mouse in the fable by that name.

Chapter Five

Pie Graphs

In these graphing activities, children organize
information into fractional parts of a circle.

The Best Time of the Year

Graph Question: *What is your favorite season?*

About the Lesson

In this activity, children paste paper figures in one of four quadrants of a circle to indicate their favorite season. While this isn't a true pie graph, it will introduce children to the circular graph form.

Making the Graph

1. Cut a large circle from the tag board.

2. Using a marker, divide the graph surface into four equal quadrants. Label each section with the name of a season. Cut the graph into four pieces.

3. Randomly divide the class into four groups. Give each group a quarter of the graph. Have groups decorate their piece of the graph with a seasonal design or motif. Reassemble the circle on a bulletin board, leaving slight spaces between each season.

4. Distribute a copy of the person pattern to each child. Tell children to decorate the pattern with clothing that reflects their favorite season. Cut the figures out.

Materials

- Tag board
- Markers
- Scissors
- Construction paper (assorted colors)
- Crayons/markers
- Person pattern (reproducible page 70)
- Glue/tape

5. Ask students to approach the graph surface one by one and glue or tape their figures onto the quadrant of the circle that represents their favorite season.

Reading the Graph •••••••••••••••••••

- Which season was selected the most? Which was selected the least? Why do you think this happened?

- Were there any seasons that were not chosen? How can we explain this?

- Which season was selected by ____ children? *(fill in a number from graph)*

- Which two seasons combine to equal _____ children? *(fill in an appropriate number)*

- Is the sum of people who prefer winter and fall greater or less than the sum who prefer spring and summer?

- Order the seasons from most to least favored.

Variation •••

You may want to take this activity one step further and have children create a true pie graph using the information on the circle graph. Create another tag-board circle, the same size as the first. Divide the circle into enough "slices" to equal the number of children in your classroom. Distribute a slice of the circle to each child. Develop a color code for the different seasons, (red for summer, yellow for fall, and so on). Have children paint their slices the appropriate color to show their favorite season. Assist children in reassembling the circle by grouping the colored slices together. Invite students to offer their ideas about how to read this graph (the largest colored section shows the season that the greatest number of students favor; the smallest section shows the season least favored). Ask children to compare the first seasonal graph they made with this one. How are the graphs similar? How are they different?

Supporting Literature

Ox Cart Man by Donald Hall (Viking Press, 1979)

The Seasons of Arnold's Apple Tree by Gail Gibbons (Harcourt, Brace, Jovanovich, 1984)

70

Pizza Party

Graph Question: *What kind of topping do you like on your pizza?*

About the Lesson

We made this pie graph showing favorite pizza toppings after reading *Little Nino's Pizzeria* by Karen Barbour. The circular shape of a pizza makes it a natural for the pie graph format. Since many children enjoy eating pizza, this graph is sure to be a popular one.

Making the Graph

1. Read aloud *Little Nino's Pizzeria* or another book about pizza. Discuss the steps and ingredients used in making pizza. Encourage children to talk about their favorite pizza toppings.

2. Cut a large circle shape from the tag board (it should be slightly smaller than the aluminum pizza tray so that it fits inside). Divide the circle into enough slices to equal the number of children in your class and cut them apart. Be sure to make the slices equal in size.

3. Distribute a tag board slice to each child. Have the children decorate the slice to show what topping they enjoy most on their pizza—pepperoni, mushrooms, meatballs, plain, and so on. (Remember, only one topping per slice.)

4. Gather the children together and have them place their slices randomly on the aluminum pizza tray. Ask students to comment on the arrangement of the slices. Can they think of a way to arrange the slices to show which toppings the most children preferred?

5. Let children move the slices around on the pizza tray until the class agrees on an arrangement. Explain that, in a pie graph, objects that are the same are

Materials

- Tag board
- Markers
- Scissors
- Aluminum pizza tray (purchased from a party store)
- Crayons

grouped together. This allows us to show which choices take up the most and least amount of room on the graph. Then we can make comparisons and answer questions.

Reading the Graph •••••••••••••

- What toppings do children like on their pizza? Can you think of any other toppings for pizza?

- Do more children like their pizza plain or with pepperoni? *(substitute other toppings to reflect your class's choices)*

- Do fewer children prefer mushrooms or meatballs on their pizza? *(substitute other toppings to reflect your class's choices)*

- Which is the most popular pizza topping? Which is the least popular?

- Are there any two toppings that children like equally well?

Variation •••••••••••••••••••••••

Here's an idea for an appealing bulletin board display. Using the pie graph format, follow the steps described on the preceding page to show students' favorite kinds of cookies. Use the reproducible cookie and cookie jar patterns on page 73 for decorative touches on a bulletin board display. (You may want to use an overhead projector to enlarge the patterns.) See pages 33 to 35 for other graphing ideas related to the theme of food.

Teaching Tips

- To evenly divide the circle for your pie graph, use the degree markings from an oversized protractor which you can probably find in an upper-grade classroom. If that is not available, enlarge your work using an opaque projector and use a regular protractor to divide the circle.

- Use the pie graph to introduce students to simple fractions as you talk about their preferences for pizza toppings. Have children use their fingers to draw imaginary lines that divide the circle into halves, then into quarters. Ask: Did more than one half of the children like their pizza with some kind of topping? Did more than a quarter of the children like pepperoni on their pizza? Did less than a quarter like mushrooms?

- Don't just talk about pizza—make it! You'll find many pizza recipes in *Pizza All Around* by Dorothy R. Colgan.

Supporting Literature

Little Nino's Pizzeria by Karen Barbour (Harcourt, Brace, Jovanovich, 1987)

How Pizza Came to Queens by Dayal Kaur Khalsa (Scholastic Inc., 1989)

Pizza All Around by Dorothy R. Colgan (Parachute Press Inc., 1992)

Cookie Jar Patterns

Shorter or Taller?

> **Graph Question:** *Are you shorter or taller than a flamingo?*

About the Lesson

Here's an offbeat but fun graph students can create to show how they measure up to an animal that they're studying. We picked a flamingo because we were doing a unit on birds, but you can use just about any animal for size comparison. This graph will help you introduce measuring and other math skills into animal studies.

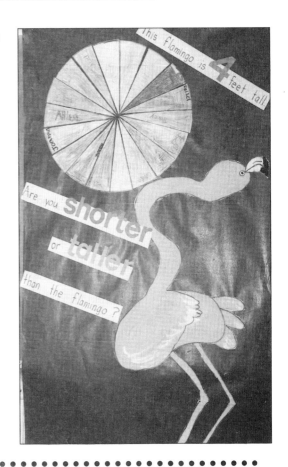

Materials

- White tag board
- Markers
- Scissors
- Mural paper
- Crayons, paints, or other drawing materials
- Tape
- Glue

Making the Graph

1. Draw a large circle on the tag board and cut it out. Cut the circle into enough slices to equal the number of children in your class.

2. Research an animal that you are currently studying to determine its height. Have the class cooperatively create a life-size drawing of that animal or enlarge a picture from a book using an opaque projector. For this graph, students painted a life-size, 4-foot flamingo.

3. Cut out the picture of the animal and tape it to a wall or chart stand. Record children's predictions as to whether they think they are taller or shorter than the animal.

4. Give each child the opportunity to stand in front of the picture to determine if he or she is taller or shorter than the animal. Discuss the results.

5. Distribute one slice of the circle to each child. Challenge children to think of how these slices can be used to show the measurement results. If no one mentions it, suggest that you pick one color to represent students who are shorter than the animal and another color to represent those who are taller. Have children color their slices accordingly.

6. Assemble children and have them arrange the slices to form a circle. See if they naturally group the colors together. If not, demonstrate how grouping the colors helps make the graph easier to read.

7. Glue the pieces of the graph onto a bulletin board or other backing.

Reading the Graph ••••••••••••••••••••••••••••••••••

- Which color was used more on our graph? What does that mean?

- Which color was used less? What does that mean?

- What would happen if someone had been the same size as the animal? How could we include this information on our graph?

- Will you always be shorter (or taller) than this animal?

Variation ••

Research the height of other animals. Children can make life-size cutouts of several different species within the same animal family. They can then use these cutouts to create a life-size graph comparing animal sizes. A few animals to try:

- Penguins — height range 16 inches to 4 feet

- Bears — height range 3 feet to 9 feet

- Dinosaurs — height range 2½ feet to 56 feet

Teaching Tip

Tall children don't always enjoy being bigger than things. Likewise, small children don't always enjoy being on the "I am smaller than" part of the graph. Structure your future graphs to include things that everyone has a chance to be smaller than (a giraffe, a sunflower) or taller than (a frog, a teddy bear).

Chapter Six

Bar Graphs

**Parallel bars of varying lengths are used to illustrate
the information being compared on these graphs.**

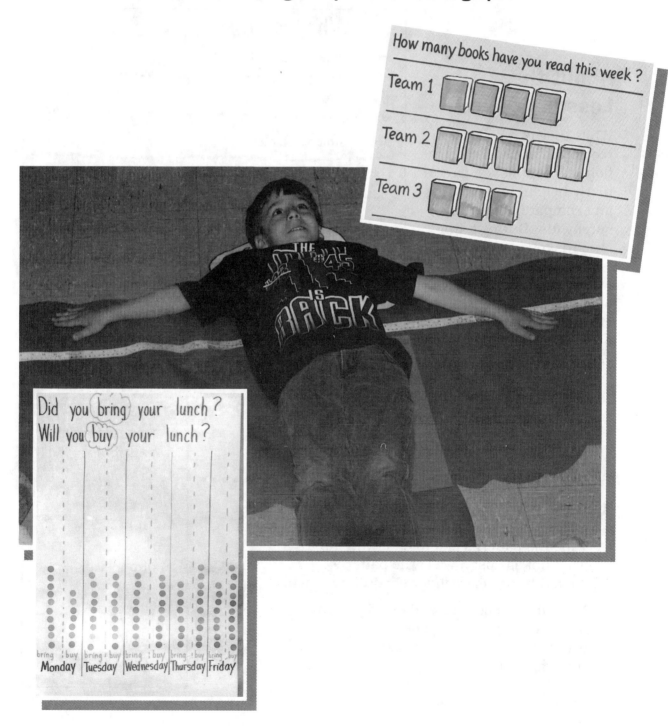

How many books have you read this week?

Team 1

Team 2

Team 3

Did you bring your lunch?
Will you buy your lunch?

bring | buy | bring | buy | bring | buy | bring | buy | bring | buy
Monday | Tuesday | Wednesday | Thursday | Friday

Spreading Out

Graph Question: *What is your arm span?*

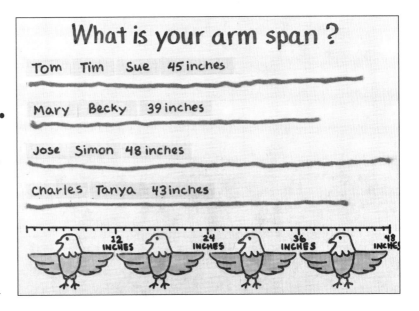

What is your arm span?

Tom Tim Sue 45 inches

Mary Becky 39 inches

Jose Simon 48 inches

Charles Tanya 43 inches

12 INCHES   24 INCHES   36 INCHES   48 INCHES

About the Lesson

While they can be used to record all kinds of information, bar graphs are particularly helpful for recording and comparing linear measurements. During a unit on birds, our students learned about the wingspan of eagles. We created this graph to help children visualize the tremendous wingspan of an eagle by comparing it with their own arm spans. This activity makes a good introduction to bar graphs, since even young children can readily make the connection between the length of the "bars" (pieces of string) and the length of their own arm spans.

Making the Graph

1. Make eight photocopies of the eagle pattern. Enlist children's help to color the birds and cut them out. Tape the patterns end to end (wing tip to wing tip) against a wall. The patterns should be low enough for children to reach.

2. Measure off one-inch and one-foot increments on the strip of paper. Tape this strip over the line of eagles to create the base of the graph.

Materials

- Eagle pattern (see reproducible page 80)
- Crayons
- Scissors
- Tape
- 8-foot strip of paper
- String
- Rulers
- Sentence strips
- Markers

3. Tell children that each of the eagle patterns is one foot wide and that the eight patterns lined up together equal the wingspan of a single eagle (8 feet, or 240 centimeters). Tell children they are going to compare their arm span to the eagle's wingspan. Ask them to make predictions about whether or not they think their arm span is less than, equal to, or greater than an eagle's.

4. Have group members take turns measuring each other's arm span using string. One child can extend his or her arms while the other two stretch a piece of string from the tip of one hand to the tip of the other. Be sure children fully extend their arms out to the side so that they are parallel to the ground.

5. Have children measure the pieces of string in inches or centimeters. Each child should then write his or her name and arm span measurement on a sentence strip.

6. Invite children to approach the graph area one by one. Tell them to line up their piece of string with the left-hand side of the measuring strip, then tape the string above the strip. Students can tape the sentence strips with their names and measurements over their respective pieces of string. Children having the same arm span measurement can tape their name labels over a single piece of string.

Teaching Tip

Children can tape together strips of construction paper to make colored bars that are the same length as their arm span. Children can use the colored strips of paper in place of the string to create a true bar graph.

Reading the Graph • • • • • • • • • • • • • • • •

- Were your predictions about your arm span correct?

- How many children have an arm span that measures more than four feet? How many have an arm span that measures less than four feet?

- What is the largest arm span in the class? What is the smallest arm span?

- Is anyone's arm span as big as an eagle's wingspan? How much bigger is the eagle's wingspan than the widest arm span in our class?

Variation •

Have children graph other body measurements like hand span (the length from the tip of the thumb to the tip of the pinky on an outstretched hand), cubit (the length from the elbow to the fingertips), or foot length.

Eagle Pattern

We Love Books!

Graph Question: *How many books have you read this week?*

About the Lesson ·········

This graph is a great way to motivate students to read. In this activity, students compile a bar graph to show how much they've read in a given week. Books can be read independently, with a buddy, or at home with a family member.

How many books have you read this week ?

Team 1

Team 2

Team 3

Making the Graph ·················

1. Divide your class into teams of three or four students.

2. To prepare the graph surface, use a marker to divide the tag board into rows. The number of rows should equal the number of teams. Make the rows wide enough to accommodate the book patterns. Label the beginning of each row with one of the team numbers (team #1, team #2, and so on).

3. Challenge students to read as many books as possible in one week. Team members can meet once a day to discuss and tally the books that they have read.

Materials

- Long sheet of butcher paper
- Markers
- Book patterns (see reproducible page 83)
- Scissors
- Crayons
- Glue or tape

4. At the end of the week, provide each team with a page of book patterns and have them cut the patterns out.

5. Assign each team a color. Ask children to color enough patterns to equal the number of books their team has read. Children should use their assigned color.

6. Invite teams to take turns approaching the graph. Each team should glue or tape its book patterns side by side (with no space between them) on the appropriate row of the graph to make a solid bar of color.

Reading the Graph •••••••••••••

- Which team read the most books?

- Which team read the least books?

- Which team read more books, team #1 or team #2? *(substitute other team numbers)*

- Which team read fewer books, team #3 or team #5? *(substitute other team numbers)*

- If you added the number of books read by teams #1 and #2, would the total be less than, more than, or equal to the number read by teams #3 and #4? *(substitute other team numbers)*

- If a team member read half a book, how would you represent it on the graph?

> ### Teaching Tip
>
> This graph is a nice activity to try during National Book Week, which falls each year on the week before Thanksgiving. Students can use art materials to replicate their favorite book jackets. Tape the jackets around the graph for a display that celebrates reading.

Variations •••

- Create a bar graph to culminate an author study. On the graph surface, list several books by the same author that children have read. Use the graph to find out which books students liked most and which they liked least.

- Have children decorate cereal boxes to resemble their favorite books. Children can then group the boxes according to genre (picturebook, biography, fairy tale, and so on). Lay the boxes on a flat surface to create a graph showing what types of books students most like to read.

Supporting Literature

Meet the Authors and Illustrators: 60 Creators of Favorite Children's Books Talk about Their Work by James Preller and Deborah Kovacs (Scholastic Professional Books, 1991) This book is for teachers.

Book Patterns

Lunch Is Served

About the Lesson

Taking the lunch count is often a part of the classroom routine. Here's a way to turn a daily chore into a meaningful math lesson.

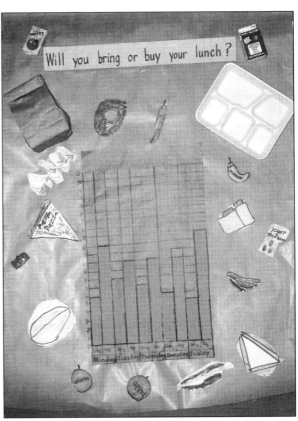

Making the Graph

1. To prepare the graph surface, make five wide columns on the tag board. Label the columns Monday through Friday to represent each day of the school week.

2. Draw a vertical line down the middle of each column to divide it in half. Write *Bring* at the top of one half of the column and *Buy* at the top of the other.

3. Draw horizontal lines across the columns to create enough boxes for each of the children in the class. Along the left side of the graph, number the boxes 0 to 25 (or higher if you have more students in your class). Move up from the base of the graph as you number the boxes.

4. Set the graph surface on an accessible table, along with two contrasting colors of paint and some paintbrushes. Assign one color for those who buy lunch on a given day and the other color for those who bring lunch. These colors should remain consistent for the entire week as children graph their lunch choices.

<table>
<tr><td colspan="2">Materials</td></tr>
<tr><td>
<ul>
<li>White tag board</li>
<li>Markers</li>
<li>Paint</li>
<li>Thin paintbrushes</li>
</ul>
</td><td></td></tr>
</table>

5. Begin the graph on a Monday. Instruct students to put a small drop of paint in a box to show whether they will bring or buy their lunch that day.

6. Select two children each day to use paint to connect the dots of the same color in each part of the column. This will create two solid bars of contrasting color. Show students how to use these bars to read the graph.

7. Each morning that follows, have the graph set up so that students can make their paint dots as soon as they arrive in class. Discuss daily and weekly totals for the *Buy* and *Bring* lunch columns.

Reading the Graph •••••••••••••••••••••••••••••••••

- Did more people bring or buy their lunch today? How do you know? *(substitute other days of the week)*

- How do we know that eight children brought their lunch on Thursday? *(fill in appropriate number and day of the week from your class's graph)*

- On what day or days did more children bring their lunch than buy it?

- On what day or days did less children bring their lunch than buy it?

- On what day did the fewer number of children bring their lunch?

- How many people brought their lunch on Monday? Did more children bring their lunch on Monday or on Tuesday? *(substitute other days of the week)*

- Did the same number of children bring and buy lunch on any day of the week? If yes, which day?

- Judging by the information on the graph, what day would you say is the most popular to buy lunch in the cafeteria?

Teaching Tip

This would be an opportune time to visit the school cafeteria to see how school lunches are prepared. Organizing a class picnic is another way to focus on lunchtime foods and related graphing activities.

Variations ••

- Continue the lunch count for several weeks, changing the form of the graph each week. For example, try a pie graph, tally graph, picture graph, and so on. (See reproducible page 86 for a lunch box pattern to use in making a picture graph.)

- Ask children to save their drink containers (soda cans, juice boxes, milk cartons) from lunch. Create an object graph showing what beverages children had at lunchtime.

Lunch Box Patterns

Graphing Across The Curriculum

This page breaks down the themes of the graphing activities in this book by curricular area.

Social Studies

- What's on Your Feet?
- Families Big and Small
- You Can Count on Wheels
- One Potato More
- Buttons Galore
- Plenty of Pockets
- Along for the Ride
- Pizza Party

Math

- Happy Birthday to Me!
- Pleasant Dreams
- Shorter or Taller?
- Spreading Out
- Lunch Is Served

Science

- Crazy About Colors
- Getting to Know You
- Left and Right
- Tooth Tally
- Who's in Our Habitat?
- Ready, Set, Sprout!
- Stuck on Stamps
- The Best Time of the Year

Language Arts

- Parts of a Name
- Lost Mittens
- A Cunning Character
- We Love Books!

NOTES